Never Worry About Retirement Again

A Financial Guide to a More Stress-Free, Happy Retirement

Aaron Campbell

authorHOUSE®

AuthorHouse™ LLC
1663 Liberty Drive
Bloomington, IN 47403
www.authorhouse.com
Phone: 1-800-839-8640

Published by AuthorHouse   09/13/2013

ISBN: 978-1-4817-5553-5 (sc)
ISBN: 978-1-4817-5552-8 (hc)
ISBN: 978-1-4817-5551-1 (e)

Library of Congress Control Number: 2013909311

ACKNOWLEDGMENTS

First, I want to thank my mom and dad. Mom, you are the most kind and motherly person I have ever met. You have always been passionate about your personal beliefs and would run through walls for your family. You have influenced thousands of lives as a teacher and librarian for 32 years. The impact you have had on my life is difficult to describe with mere words.

Dad, you are the most respected, moral, ethical, gentle, yet powerful man I have encountered in my lifetime. You always taught me to be honest, even when no one was watching. You taught me to do the "right" thing not just the "easy" thing. And you taught me that there is generally a "price" for anything good in life, and only a few will pay the price required to achieve what they want.

I also want to thank my wife, Cherie. Thank you for your understanding and unconditional support. You are a wonderful mother and friend and I look forward to all the exciting things that the future holds.

To the clients of Campbell Financial Services, Inc., thank you for your trust in me to be your financial guide. I am committed to your success and helping you become more stress free and happy during your retirement years.

A special thank you goes to my in-laws, Mark and Tina. Thank you for believing in me and encouraging me to follow my entrepreneurial spirit. Without your support Campbell Financial Services would probably not be here today.

Also, I would like to thank all the professionals and support staff I have had the opportunity to learn from over the last ten years. Thank you to Mike Martin for introducing me to an entirely different way of helping families protect their life savings and for being a good friend and business mentor. Finally, thank you to all the friends and family who have supported me throughout my life. Thank you all!

Never Worry About Retirement Again

A Financial Guide to a
More Stress-Free, Happy Retirement

TABLE OF CONTENTS

INTRODUCTION

Today we live in an ever-changing, fast-paced, hectic world. In the past one hundred years, we've seen some of the greatest advancements in history. What a privilege it is to be living in such a prosperous time. Just think about the things we enjoy today that our ancestors could have only dreamed about. We have cell phones, high-definition TVs, the Internet, airplanes, automobiles, electricity, indoor plumbing, McDonald's, and Walmart. We have even sent human beings to the moon.

However, despite all the luxuries and technologies we have around us, life itself can be a very challenging experience. Most people go through similar phases in their lives and experience similar things along the way. I categorize the four phases of life as follows:

1. *Childhood* (play, eat, sleep)

2. *Working years* (save money)

3. *Pre-Retirement* (Am I doing the right things? Can I afford to quit my job?)

4. *Retirement* (relying on saved money to provide income)

Childhood starts at birth and continues until our late teens. This phase of life is generally great. The main activities during this time are playing, going to school, eating, and sleeping. I find it fascinating to watch my seven-year-old son when the mailman comes to deliver the mail. He always yells, "Daddy, Daddy, what did I get in the mail?" As he's saying this, I always think, *I don't know why you're so excited about getting the mail. There's nothing but bills.* But he is expecting a birthday card (normally with money in it) or an invitation to a party or some other fun thing. What a great time of life!

However, before we know it, childhood evolves into adulthood, and we must start the working phase of our life. We have to get a job so we can put a roof over our head and food on the table. This is where life really begins. We all have a wide-open world to do and become whatever it is that we want. However, there can be roadblocks and challenges along the way. The responsibility is on us to make it and to survive. This generally is a period when people experience a high level of stress. Just think about all the responsibilities:

- Student loans and credit card debt

- Mortgage

- Car payments

- Life insurance

- Health care costs

- Vacations

- Flat-screen TVs, phone, etc.

- Saving for kids' college funds

- Saving for retirement

During this phase, it is very easy to become overwhelmed. Sometimes it seems like there is no light at the end of the tunnel. I find more and more people today are having a difficult time trying to maintain their lifestyles while still preparing for the next phase of life. However, if you have made good decisions and have been disciplined, at some point you will enter into the pre-retirement phase.

Pre-retirement is the five to ten years before you quit your job. It is critical to make good financial decisions during this phase. This is the time that will ultimately make or break your retirement. If there was ever a time to become more educated and more cautious, this is it. This is also the most exciting time in life for many people, as they can just start to see the light at the end of the work tunnel. If they make the right decisions, they can be on their way to a stress-free, happy retirement. However, if they make the wrong decisions, they could be on their way to extending their working years.

Retirement is the final phase of life. That simply means that you rely on no one other than yourself to provide an acceptable quality of life. That means no more work. Most people spend an entire lifetime accumulating assets so someday they are able to do whatever they want whenever they want. This phase of life should be like being a kid. Play, eat, and sleep!

The purpose of this book is to help people better understand how to become successful, prosperous, and financially independent so they can enjoy life to the fullest. My goal is to reduce all of the technical and sophisticated-sounding financial theories into easy-to-understand, easy-to-implement steps that will drastically increase the probability of achieving financial freedom and ultimately enjoying a more stress-free, happy retirement.

CHAPTER 1

Laying a Foundation

"Financial success is reserved for those who aggressively seek financial knowledge and then apply that knowledge to create a prosperous life."

Aaron Campbell

Have you ever wondered why some people are successful and why some people are not? Maybe you know someone who was raised almost identically to you, had the same educational background, and made a similar amount of money. Yet they may have achieved a much higher level of financial success than you. Is it because they got lucky? Is it because they worked harder than you? Is it because they were smarter than you?

I have found that success often has nothing to do with ability level or desire. Most people seem to have the desire to do better and most have the ability to achieve more, so what is the secret? What is the recipe for financial success?

To get started, you must lay a foundation that will be wide enough and strong enough on which to build your personal financial empire. I have found that there are seven simple steps to building a strong financial foundation that will support a life of financial freedom.

Seven Simple Steps to Building a Strong Financial Foundation

1. Educate yourself about how money works.

2. Pay yourself before you pay any other person or company.

3. Do *not* spend more than you make.

4. Pay off debt as quickly as possible.

5. Invest the money you pay yourself so it will provide a future income and will not be lost.

6. Buy insurance to protect the things you cannot afford to lose.

7. Trust yourself to make a good decision.

1. Educate Yourself

It is absolutely astounding that most of our children are not taught in school about finance or how money works. Isn't the ability to earn more money and to become more financially secure one of the main reasons we go to school in the first place? Yet most Americans end up using the trial and error method when making financial decisions.

I know it can be intimidating with all the financial mumbo jumbo out there. It can also be intimidating to go to a financial advisor or financial person that may look at you as if you are a second-class citizen if you do not have a million dollars to invest. However, educating yourself about how money works is probably the most profitable investment of time and effort you will ever make. So in this chapter I want to talk in simple, straightforward terms and provide simple, easy-to-understand truths that apply to almost everyone. I also hope to provide some good financial education along the way.

2. Pay Yourself First

The second key and probably one of the most basic ideas is to simply pay yourself before you pay anyone else. What I mean by paying yourself first is simply saving a portion of whatever you make right off the top before you pay anyone else. The money you pay yourself should be invested with the purpose of providing a future income that will ultimately replace the income you make by working. Think about some of the people and companies you could pay before you pay yourself:

- Mortgage company

- Electric company

- Gas company

- Phone company

- Grocery store

- Clothing store

- Car finance companies

- Restaurant

- Movie theater

- Cafe

- And others

I realize we have to spend money to live; we must purchase goods and services. But there is no company or person that is more important to pay than yourself. If you never pay yourself, how will you ever have anything? Many people tell me that they don't have any extra money to pay themselves every month. My reply is, "Baloney!" You must pay yourself first, and if you don't have enough money left at the end of the month, consider reducing your expenses or find a way to make more money.

It has been said that most good things in life require some type of sacrifice and some level of discipline. This is what typically separates those who have financial success and those who don't. If you asked two people who worked for the same company, made the same amount of money, and worked the same hours if they felt they could afford to save money before they paid their bills, their answer might be, "No." Yet one of those employees may have five children and the other may be single with no children. Wouldn't you think that the single person would have a much better chance of saving money than the person with five children? People tend to spend whatever they make. That's why it is absolutely crucial to pay yourself before any other person or company.

3. Do *Not* Spend More Than You Make

I know this sounds like common sense, but it is very difficult for most people. Not spending more than you make means just that: do not spend more than you make. That means you pay yourself at least five to ten percent right off the top. Then you will use ninety to ninety-five percent of the rest of your income to establish your lifestyle.

Today too many people want to live lifestyles that require more money than they actually bring in each month. That is a recipe for disaster. Consider this saying: *"Successful and prosperous people are willing to live a temporary lifestyle that most will not so someday they can enjoy a lifestyle that most cannot."*

4. Pay Off Debt As Quickly As You Can

If you owe money to a company or another person, you will probably have to pay interest for the privilege of using the borrowed money. Though I understand it is sometimes necessary to borrow money, perhaps to buy a house or a car, I have found that most successful people have paid off debt as soon as possible. That way the interest they were paying to make someone else rich goes back in their pockets to build their own wealth.

There are many calculations that can be made to determine whether or not it is a good idea to pay off a mortgage or other debt early. However, in almost every situation, if you choose to pay off debt as fast as you can, you will not only be happier, but you will end up having more money.

Now, there are exceptions to this rule that I cannot ignore. For example, my best friend has never made very much money from employment. He had four children, and his wife stayed home with the kids. Yet he was able to purchase his first home using a loan from the bank. A couple of years later he had to relocate, and instead of selling his current home, he found that he could rent the home for more than his payment to the bank every month.

When he did this, light bulbs went off in his head that he could make money by borrowing money. If he could borrow money with a five-hundred-dollar per month payment and collect seven hundred dollars a month for rent, he could effectively make two hundred dollars a month that he didn't have to work for. Today he has over forty properties. In the next five years, he will have a few of the forty houses paid for and will be making approximately twelve thousand dollars a month in rental income. Though he still has maintenance expenses and taxes to pay from the rental income, the income he gets to keep he didn't have to go to work to get. And the best part is that he used very little of his own money to provide this income.

My friend would have never been able to reach this financial position by saving a little money off the top of his paycheck every month. Yet, by educating himself and borrowing money with a strategic future purpose, he has been able to do very well. Just keep in mind that though this is possible, it requires a significant amount of time and risk to make it work. Just educate yourself and consider if you would be happy using debt to help build your future assets or not.

So now you have begun educating yourself about money; you have started paying yourself every month before paying anyone else; you are living within your means; and you are paying your debt as soon as possible. Something miraculous is going to start to happen: You are going to find that you're accumulating money. It is almost magical the first time you realize that you are actually doing it. You are making progress toward financial security and peace of mind, and it is exciting. It is liberating!

5. Invest the Money You Pay Yourself

Start using your saved money to grow and produce more money for your future. The money you pay yourself every month is someday going to be used to replace the income you receive from working. Therefore, it must be a priority to invest in areas that will produce a constant, reliable income in the future. There are many different places where you can invest money.

- Stocks

- Bonds

- Real estate

- Commodities

- Personal businesses

- Annuities

- Cash value life insurance

- Real Estate Investment Trust

- Private capital investments

- And others

The key to making good financial decisions and picking the right type of investments is educating yourself and seeking advice from professionals who understand and specialize in the area you are interested in using to grow your savings. I will address methods of investing and growing dollars in later chapters.

6. Buy Insurance

You need to protect the things you cannot afford to lose. In December of 2012, the area where I live experienced an ice storm that took down thousands of trees, and left people across the state without electrical power. The electricity at my house went out on Christmas night and stayed off for several days. It was very cold outside, and we had about six inches of snow on the ground. But we have a wood-burning fireplace in our home, so we just made a nice fire to help keep us warm. Since we had no electricity, we went outside, took our son sledding, and made snow ice cream. Then we came home and warmed up hot chocolate right on the fire. It was a really fun day.

At about ten o'clock that evening, as we were about to go to bed, I threw a couple of pieces of wood in the fireplace, and we bundled a bunch of blankets on the beds to try to stay warm as the temperature was down in the low twenties outside. My wife looked like a mummy. She had on two pairs of sweatpants, two pairs of socks, two or three shirts, and about three blankets. I told her she was going to get hot and would sweat under all of that clothing, but she didn't care; she just wanted to get warm.

Around midnight she woke up (because she was hot) and started taking off the top layers of clothing. Then she heard something popping in the living room and woke me up. "Get up and go see what's popping!" she said. Well, it was about forty degrees in the house and I was quite warm under the mountain of blankets, so I said, "It is just the cold wood popping in the fireplace. It's normal."

My wife kept asking me to check; she is quite persistent when she wants something done. So I said, "Okay, okay, I'll go look." I walked into the living room and looked at the fireplace. The wood was burning normally, but I could hear a weird popping noise. I figured the popping was just the ice outside making branches on the trees snap. So, I walked back into the bedroom and reported to my wife that everything looked fine.

Then I happened to notice a light flickering on the snow outside. Immediately I thought the power had been restored. I went to the light switch and flicked it on, but nothing happened. I walked over to the French doors in our bedroom, opened them, and walked out on our deck to see where the light was coming from. It was coming from our chimney, which was *on fire*. I screamed at my wife to get up and get dressed, because the house was on fire.

We ran around in circles trying to find clothes and shoes in the dark. I grabbed the phone and tried to call 911, while she got our son out of bed and bundled him in a blanket. I then drove them to a neighbor's house. I got back to our house quickly and got a wheelbarrow that I had used to move firewood from the firewood pile to the house.

My mind immediately told me to get pictures and keepsakes— the things that couldn't be replaced due to sentimental value. So I started grabbing everything I could get my hands on and throwing it into the wheelbarrow. I got pictures and clothes and guitars— whatever I could think of in the time I had before the fire became too dangerous.

The fire department showed up and started working to put out the fire. As I stood in the snow, watching my home begin to break down, I started to think about what the next steps would be. Where would we go, what would we do, and so on. Though the logistics of what would happen were unclear to me at the time, I was peaceful knowing that my family and our most important sentimental items were safe and that we had *insurance*.

We pay a relatively small amount of money monthly to an insurance company to provide protection of an asset we can't afford to lose. Now, I am human, and I don't like to pay premiums for insurance that I think I may never use. However, when we do need the protection, the value of insurance becomes evident. Our insurance company literally took care of us during this time.

Buying insurance does not just apply to a home. Think about your retirement savings and the sacrifice and time it takes to accumulate. Now think about saving for twenty years or more and then having a major catastrophe (such as a stock market crash). Your life savings would be destroyed. Wouldn't that be a lot like watching your home burn? But instead of feeling a wave of relief, knowing you were going to be saved by your insurance company, you would have terrible dread, knowing you had no protection, no safety net for one of your largest assets.

Wouldn't it have made sense to simply protect your savings from loss, just as you would with your home? If you understand the importance of this principle and will follow this rule, your level of stress in your retirement years will decrease and your level of happiness will increase. You will no longer have to worry that today may be the day you lose your assets.

Often people make financial mistakes due to lack of education. Once they make a mistake and lose money, a sense of urgency amplifies the problem. This leads to more mistakes. Emotions coupled with impatience lead people to seek out faster, easier ways to make money, like get-rich-quick schemes. They end up taking risks in unproven areas without ensuring the safety and ultimate return of their money. This is how financial catastrophes happen. When you place the things you can't afford to lose at risk, the outcome generally will not be favorable. In the game of planning for a stress-free, happy retirement, *not* losing *is* winning.

7. Trust Yourself

There is no one on Earth who cares more about you than you. If you have educated yourself, have followed the other six financial keys, and have sought advice from experts, then make a decision not to worry about making mistakes. Though mistakes will happen, and you may make some bad choices, as long as you follow these principles, your probability for success is very, very high. So now you have the keys to building a prosperous financial future.

Next, I will get much more specific about the challenges that you may face in the future. I will also talk about some history and about specific plans to help you plan for and enjoy a stress-free, happy retirement.

CHAPTER 2

The *Shift/Shaft*

"Neither a wise nor a brave man lies down
on the tracks of history to wait for the
train of the future to run over him."

Dwight D. Eisenhower

The path to retirement was much different in the past than it is today. You may have had parents or grandparents who worked the same job at the same company for their entire lives. They were dedicated to the company because they were working toward a company pension. (A pension is a promised lifetime payment a company pays to an employee as a retirement benefit for his or her years of service.) They simply worked hard and stayed dedicated to their company. And when they hit retirement age, they got a guaranteed paycheck for the rest of their lives. In recent years some companies that provided pension benefits to retired employees have had financial difficulty. However, the Employee Retirement Income Security Act of 1974 created an independent agency of the United States government called the Pension Benefit Guarantee Corporation (PBGC). This agency program was created to protect retired employees that were promised pension payments from their companies. Today if a company has financial difficulty and can no longer make the promised payments to their retired workers, the PBGC would take over to continue paying the promised payments up to a specified maximum. In life there are no absolute guarantees. However, when it comes to retirement income, company pension payments are typically considered a very stable form of retirement income.

Just think about how enjoyable retirement must have been. Every single month, two paychecks would come in the mail: one from the company pension plan and one from Social Security. What a great time in history for retirees! However, all good things generally come to an end. In 1978 something took place that would have a huge impact on the way we would look at retirement. I call it the great shift/shaft. Most companies did away with company pension plans and replaced those plans with what we now call the 401k plan.

The 401k would become the replacement for most pension plans in America, placing the responsibility for providing retirement income back on the employee. That's why I call it the *shaft*. You see, a 401k is simply an account set up by an employer that gives the employee the ability to save for retirement. The employee can have a portion of his or her paycheck automatically deposited into the 401k each month. The money deposited into this account is sheltered from current income taxes. That means that the employee doesn't have to pay any income tax on the savings or the interest on that account until they pull the money out.

This idea made great sense in the 1970s because a married couple with a taxable income of fifty thousand dollars a year would have been in a 51 percent tax bracket. The premise was that a family could shelter some of its income in the 401k, and when they retired, they would have less income and hopefully less taxes.

Well, the 401k rapidly became the main source of retirement savings for the largest generation in the history of the world, called the Baby Boom Generation. The Baby Boom was a generational glitch that occurred due to the massive increase in the birthrate between 1946 and 1964.

So, by the early 1980s, a tsunami of new money was being saved in 401k plans by the nearly 76 million Baby Boomers. This started a twenty-year period of unprecedented growth in our country and around the world. You see, most 401k plans invested in stocks and bonds. Therefore, massive amounts of money were flowing into the market, leading to a very exciting ride for the Boomer generation for the next twenty years.

The Boomers' experience over the next two decades would be historic. According to data collected from www.dowjones.com, the Dow Jones Industrial Average from November 1982 to January 2000 had a cumulative return of 1003.19 percent, or an annualized return of 15.09 percent. Think about the effect this would have on the world. The people accumulating money to replace their pensions in the '80s and '90s were having great success. They were enjoying significant tax savings and benefiting from double-digit returns for the majority of their working careers. This was considered to be normal.

So the Boomer generation was the first generation to be mostly without company pension plans. It was their responsibility to save money and invest that money so it could provide an income for them in the future. The majority of this generation had no formal investment training and no real guidance on how to make investment decisions in stocks and bonds. Yet the majority of most people's retirement money was tied to the stock market in one way or the other.

This process worked great until the year 2000. In 2000, the earliest Boomers were in their mid-fifties and could see the light at the end of the work tunnel. Remember, most of them had no pensions to look forward to but they did have 401k accounts that had done very well for the previous twenty years. Then the world started to change. In the early 2000s, we saw the "Tech Bubble" burst which resulted in massive losses on Wall Street. Then we saw the terrible day of September 11, 2001, when our country was devastatingly attacked by terrorist.

At this time, when people needed to be assured that their money was safe and everything was going to be okay, the stock market closed and did not open again for seven days—the longest closure since the Great Depression. When the market reopened, the Dow Jones Industrial Average fell 7.1 percent—the biggest one-day point drop in history. If you had money in the stock market then, you remember the emotions you felt as you saw your life's savings rapidly decline at the time you needed it the most.

This was the start of what many have called the New Normal. In the last ten years, we have seen the housing bubble burst, hundred-year-old companies go belly up, and trillions of tax dollars go to bail out companies deemed "too big to fail." Our stock market has been extremely volatile, and interest rates continue to be very low. Our most sacred programs, such as Social Security and Medicare, are woefully underfunded, and the economy is looking bleak.

So the bottom line is this: things are different today than they were in the '80s and '90s. That means now is the time to get serious about planning and educating yourself so you can ensure a stress-free, happy retirement, no matter what the economy throws at you.

CHAPTER 3

Investor? Worker? Protector? What Are You?

"As you become more clear about who you really are, you'll be better able to decide what is best for you—the first time around."

Oprah Winfrey

Trying to determine who you really are in life can be a challenging task. I remember being a young child, maybe seven or eight, watching everything that my dad did. He was a basketball coach and teacher at a very small school district in Arkansas. When I say small, I mean there were 410 people in the entire town. Whenever there was a game, everyone in the town would show up to support their team.

Everyone knew my dad; everyone knew him as Coach Campbell. I used to think he was famous because everyone wanted to talk to him and shake his hand. So, for as long as I could remember, I always wanted to be just like my dad. I would try to walk like Dad and talk like Dad and laugh like Dad and dress like Dad and basically become just like my dad. Even today I notice myself comparing who I am or how I make decisions to Dad. I was fortunate to have such a positive role model.

However, as an adult I have come to realize that just because Dad did something a certain way or made decisions a certain way or invested money a certain way, that didn't mean that was the way *I* needed to do things. My life and my experiences are unique to me, and I must make decisions based on my strengths and weaknesses instead of doing what Dad did. So, self-awareness is a key attribute to making good financial decisions.

When it comes to money and investments, it's important to know who you are and who you are not. Assuming you have taken the steps outlined in Chapter 1, and you have accumulated some assets, you may find that you fall into one of three categories:

1. Investment masters

2. Workers

3. Protectors

It's important to figure out which of these categories you fall into so you can make good decisions about how to grow your money for the future.

Investment Masters

An investment master is someone who has saved money, and now wants to grow that money as fast as possible while taking the least amount of risk. This is someone who has invested significant amounts of time learning about the area where he or she is potentially going to invest money. Most true investment masters are able to answer basic yet critical questions, such as

- Do you know how your investment works?

- Do you know the fees in your investment?

- Do you know how much risk your investment has?

- Do you know what the maximum returns could be with your investment?

- Do you understand why you own this investment?

- Do you know how this investment will help you reach your overall goals?

A true successful investment master knows the answers to these questions and generally does not need a financial advisor or planner to help guide him or her into good investments. Being an investment master requires a great deal of study, reading, and research. Even then the most seasoned, educated investors can lose money from time to time. However, they know the level of risk and the possibility of return before investing. I admire the investment masters of the world because they use their own time and effort to research and learn about the areas they want to invest. The ultimate responsibility of making money or losing money falls directly on them.

I do, however, encourage the investment masters to set up a transition plan that clearly spells out what steps should be taken if they become incapacitated and can no longer manage their affairs. I think about my mother, for example. She is a very, very smart person, but she has no interest in taking care of financial matters. She simply relies on my father to take care of the family's finances. So what happens if something happens to my father? Well, luckily I will be there to help my mother continue my father's plans, but what if I'm not there to help her? I am afraid she will simply be overwhelmed. That's why it is wise to build a relationship with a financial professional to build a plan to carry out your wishes if you are not able to.

Workers

Workers are those with little to no formal training or education about the area in which they are willing to invest. Workers generally rely on advice from friends or coworkers, or they just "wing it" and hope everything works out. Workers could also include people who *do* have an understanding of how investments work, but they don't have the time or desire to research and make decisions about their investments. They value the advice of outside advisors regarding financial matters.

A great example of a worker would be someone with a job that offers a 401k plan. Generally a 401k plan provides anywhere from ten to fifty investment options. Normally these are mutual funds that invest in either stocks or bonds. The employee has the responsibility of choosing which investment is going to be best for his or her situation. I have met hundreds of people in my career who have 401k plans. I would guess that ninety percent of the people with a 401k have absolutely no idea which investment option to choose. I can't say that I blame the employee.

You see, generally there is very little education for employees when it comes to what investments to pick that will match their goals. They know that they need to save money, and they are doing what they think they need to do. But it is alarming that people save hundreds, if not thousands, of dollars every month in an investment they know nothing about. Think about this: you sacrifice and save money so someday you won't have to work anymore. Wouldn't you want to provide it as much protection as possible? After all, isn't that saved money going to help take care of you in the future?

When I see people invest such significant amounts of money in places they know very little about, I want to help educate them so they can make better decisions. They generally have no desire to become an investment master, so they need education and guidance. If they get neither, it's likely that their money will treat them only as well as they treated it along the way. If you feel like you want to become a better steward of your money, either educate yourself or find a qualified financial advisor.

Protectors

Protectors save their money very conservatively. Their main concern is simply not losing money. This type of person might save money at home in the freezer or bury money in the backyard. Protectors normally save money, live on less than they make, and have little or no debt. They don't have any desire to take risks with their money in order to make fantastic returns; they simply don't want to lose.

However, many protectors have started looking for places they can save money that has better growth potential than a bank CD. Current CD rates are very low. A one-year CD is paying less than half a percent per year. Protectors know that this is bad news for them because that percentage doesn't come close to keeping pace with inflation.

You are likely to fall into one of the previous three categories. You are either an educated, seasoned investment master who doesn't need outside help. You are a hard-working person who is simply trying to save and grow your money, but you don't have the time or desire to become an investment master. Or you are a protector—a conservative saver who has no interest in taking risk but still wants to make as much interest as possible.

In the following chapters, I'll discuss my philosophy of how to provide a stress-free, happy retirement, no matter what type of person you are.

CHAPTER 4

How the Game Is Played

"When you know better you do better."

Maya Angelou

Have you ever played a video game with a child or grandchild? My seven-year-old son always wants me to play video games with him. He thinks I should be a great video-game player, defeating any opponent and getting over every obstacle in the game. You see, he looks at me like I am a grownup, and he figures that I must be more skilled at a simple game than a little kid like him.

So I go into his room to play a video game with him, and he is so excited that Dad is going to be awesome at the game. Well, I grab the controller, and I start the game. About thirty seconds into the game, I am dead. I don't even make it a minute. My son then says, "Okay, it's my turn, Dad." Well, about thirty minutes later he is still playing and telling me about all the secret worlds and weapons and traps and the different good guys and bad guys. He is seven; I am an adult. I am bigger and stronger than he, yet he is easily able to outperform me in this video game.

You see, my son had something I did not: experience. He had played that game many times; he knew all the rules; he knew all the enemies; and he knew all the weapons that were available to help him be successful. I simply didn't have his experience.

Investing money throughout your lifetime is a lot like playing a game. There are weapons or tools (stocks, bonds, mutual funds, real estate, and so on) that can be used to help accomplish your objective. Each level has different challenges and different enemies (inflation, market volatility, taxes, insurance costs, and so on) that must be conquered. How you invest your savings will depend on your current phase of life.

So, before we go any further, let's talk about a few general investments and saving tools that are at your disposal to help grow money. I like to segment these tools into two main categories:

1. Risky

2. Safe

Risky Investments

I define *risky* as any investment that fluctuates in value. In other words, it has the ability to increase in value or decrease in value, based on market conditions. There are many different types of investments that we could consider risky:

1. Stocks

2. Bonds

3. Mutual funds

4. Real Estate
   Investment Trusts (REIT)

> **Characteristics of Risky Investments**
>
> - Principal is *not* guaranteed.
> - Interest/earnings are not guaranteed.
> - Terms are generally open ended.
> - They may need an extended amount of *time* to be effective.
>
> Potential Earnings/Losses:
> UNLIMITED

5. Gold

6. Municipal bonds

7. Real estate

8. Variable annuities

9. And others

Many people in the working phase of life are exposed to these risky investment options. Most people have some type of retirement account at work such as a 401k, TSP, or 403b. However, if you don't want to save into your company's retirement account, there are accounts you can set up with outside companies called brokerage accounts. These accounts allow you to purchase stocks, bonds, mutual funds, and many other types of investments.

Most of the time younger people are encouraged to take more risks in an attempt to make more interest. The theory is that if an investment decreases in value over a short period, young people should not be concerned because they still have time to weather the storm and continue saving and investing normally.

In general, there are three ways investment accounts can be set up. The main difference between the three options is the type of service you receive and how you pay for that service.

1. Discount brokerage company

2. Full-service brokerage company

3. Discount brokerage with professional management

Discount brokerage companies are designed for the do-it-yourselfer or the investment master. They allow an investor to buy or sell investments at a discounted commission. Some firms can offer commission rates as low as five to ten dollars per trade to buy or sell an investment. This type of account makes trading individual stocks affordable for the investor who doesn't need any guidance.

Full-service brokerage companies provide a large variety of services for their clients. They provide research, retirement planning, tax information, and many more services supplied by an assigned representative. However, these extra services may come with a significant price tag. At a full-service brokerage company, you could pay commissions of forty dollars or more per trade. Commissions are generated only when transactions are made. Therefore, it is up to you to trust that the broker is making buy or sell recommendations for the right reasons and not just to generate commissions.

Discount brokerage companies with professional management are just like the discount brokerage companies above, but there will generally be a professional advisor who provides a customized portfolio based on your long-term goals. They manage that portfolio and make changes as needed. This type of management is fee based, as opposed to commission based. *Fee based* simply means that instead of being paid commissions, the manager is paid a fee (generally based on a percentage of the account.) Some transaction charges may be imposed by the broker dealer or custodian holding the account in addition to the fees charged by the investment advisor. If your portfolio makes money, your manager makes money. If your portfolio loses money, your manager would also make less money. Therefore, if your money manager makes a recommendation to buy or sell something, you can bet that he or she is making the recommendation to benefit you and not just to generate a commission.

In recent years, many people have been abandoning full-service brokerage companies and money managers and moving their money to discount brokerage companies. Many people who used full-service brokerage companies and money managers were paying fees and commissions for research and advice and still lost their shirts two times in the 2000s, once in 2000–2002 and again in 2007–2009.

If you are going to pay a fee or a commission for people to help you with your investments, you must make sure that they can justify why you should pay them for their help. What makes them valuable? What is it about their recommendation that is going to make your situation better? How are they different from everyone else? Do they understand you and what you want for the future? Do they know what the purpose of the money is?

I believe it's very important to understand what a financial professional's motivation is and how he or she is paid. Though the financial industry is mostly made up of excellent, ethical professionals, it pays to educate yourself on how each of these organizations makes money. It may also be helpful to review your broker's professional background by going to www.finra.org. Then you can decide what is right for you and your situation.

Safe Savings Places

In recent years, some people have completely abandoned the stock market and brokerage companies and instead are concerned with the safety of their money. These people may be interested in the second category of investments: safe savings places. You see, an investment goes up and down in value, but a savings account never decreases in value due to market fluctuations. I have found only three places that top experts would consider to be safe savings accounts:

> **Characteristics of Safe Investments**
>
> - Principal is guaranteed
> - Minimum interest is guaranteed
> - Penalties charged for early withdrawals.
> - Specific term used.
>
> Potential Earnings/Losses:
> LIMITED

1. Banks: deposits covered by FDIC

2. Government bonds: held to maturity

3. Insurance companies: fixed and fixed indexed annuities

To explain the basic concept of how these types of accounts work, I like to use a basic bank CD as an example. In a bank CD, you deposit money for a set amount of time or term (such as one year) and a set rate of interest (such as one percent). When the time or term is up, your principal and interest is returned to you. There are no fees or commissions that you pay out-of-pocket, and if you remain within the FDIC insurance limits, your money is deemed to be safe, even if the bank were to go out of business.

Government bonds also have a set term and a set interest rate, and as long as they are held until the end of the term, they are considered to be guaranteed. Though not FDIC insured, they are backed by the full faith and credit of the United States government.

Then we have fixed-annuity products issued by insurance companies. In very general terms, a fixed annuity is a deposit with an insurance company instead of a bank. The insurance company then pays a fixed interest rate for a fixed time.

It is worthwhile to note that many people confuse fixed annuities with variable annuities in terms of safety. I have met many people who have owned variable annuities that have seen large decreases in value in the last decade. The variable annuity is the only type of annuity that would fall into the risky category explained previously. So be advised that *fixed* annuities are safe, and *variable* annuities are risky. I will talk about safety in greater detail in the next chapter.

We have talked about how to set up investment accounts and about the general categories of risk and safety. Now it is important to talk about how different types of accounts are taxed.

TAXABLE NOW	TAXABLE LATER	TAXABLE NEVER
• Savings/ checking • CD's • Mutual Funds (NQ) • Brokerage Accts. (NQ)	• IRAs • 401k • 403b • TSA • Annuity interest	• Roth IRA • Municipal bonds • Certain types of life insurance
The interest made in each of these accounts is generally taxable at the end of every year. Even if you do not withdraw the interest, you will still receive a 1099 for any interest earned and will owe tax.	*Generally 100 percent of the money in these types of account is not subject to tax during the savings or accumulation phase. However, they will be taxed at your highest tax rate when withdrawn.*	*Any interest made in these type of accounts will never be taxed. It is tax free. Certain conditions apply.*

Let's think of the three tax categories as buckets where we can store money. For example, if you have a 401k, you could go to the chart above to determine how your 401k will be taxed. So, if you have $100,000 in your 401k that means you have *never* paid taxes on *any* of that amount. Therefore, whenever you withdraw money from the account, you will owe tax on one hundred percent of the withdrawal. Also note that the money withdrawn will be taxed at your highest tax rate.

Another example would be a savings account at your local bank. According to the chart above, any interest you make will be taxable every year, regardless of whether you take the money out or not.

It's very important to know the different types of accounts and how each is taxed because it is not how much interest you make that matters; it is how much interest you get to keep. I have people ask me all the time, "Hey, Aaron, what are those ROTH IRAs paying nowadays?" The answer to that question is that a ROTH IRA is just a type of account; it is what type of investment you put inside the ROTH IRA account that determines how much interest it might make.

For example, if you were a person who wanted to invest in *risky* investments, you could open a ROTH IRA with a *discount* brokerage company and buy stocks or bonds or mutual funds to put inside that ROTH account. If the investments you chose made money, then according to the chart above, you would not owe any taxes on the gains. Because your investment was in a ROTH IRA account, the interest made is tax free. In today's world, with government spending and debt at all-time highs, many believe that taxes will certainly increase in the future. If you believe that taxes will go up, would you rather pay taxes now (while taxes are low) or later (when taxes may be higher)? That is your decision to make, and it is your decision what type of account you want to use to save and grow your money.

In summary, it is absolutely crucial to become proficient in how the basics of the money game are played. Here's a summary:

1. Places to go to invest money with exposure to market risk

    a. Discount brokerage

    b. Full-service brokerage

    c. Discount brokerage with professional management

2. Places to go to invest money with some type of protection

    a. Bank

    b. Government

    c. Insurance companies (fixed annuities)

3. Three ways different accounts are taxed

    a. Taxable now

    b. Taxable later

    c. Taxable never (Certain conditions apply)

CHAPTER 5

Tools of the Trade

Have you ever seen a child try to use a tool for the first time? When my son was about four, I was working on a little project in the garage that required a hammer and a screwdriver. This was a simple project that came complete with instructions of when to use nails and when to use screws. My son wanted to help with this project at a time when the instructions were calling for nails. I told him to grab a nail and nail it to the board as indicated in the instructions.

When I handed him the nail, he lined it up on the board, grabbed the screwdriver, and started stabbing away at the head of the nail. I screamed, "Son! You're going to stab yourself trying to nail that nail with a screwdriver. Use the hammer!"

"What's a hammer?" he asked. He didn't know what either tool was or what they were designed to do. He just picked up a tool and started jabbing.

Many times people treat investment tools the same way. This can cause serious problems. Just as my son could have stabbed himself trying to use a screwdriver to nail a nail, many people can suffer serious problems by using a tool that doesn't match the goal they are trying to accomplish. So in this chapter we will look deeper into four basic types of investments that most people are likely to use in their lifetime:

1. CDs

2. Bonds

3. Stock market

4. Annuities

CDs

At the time this book was being written, the average one-year bank CD was paying 0.77 percent interest per year. To put that into perspective, if you deposited $100,000 in a one-year CD over the course of the year, the bank would pay you $770 or $64 per month. If you had $500,000 invested in that same one-year CD, you would receive $3,850 or $320 per month in retirement income. Do you think that is a good deal for you? Although the CD is considered to be safe from market volatility, the tiny amount of interest made does not buy a lot.

Bonds

In a search for higher interest, many people have gravitated toward the bond market. A bond is simply an agreement between an investor and a corporation or municipality in which the investor (you) agrees to lend money to that organization for a specific time period. The company then agrees to pay you a specified rate of interest for that period.

For example, if you lent $100,000 to XYZ Company for twenty years at five percent interest, the company would issue you a bond (IOU).

The company would then start paying you $5,000 per year interest for the next twenty years. At the end of the term, the company would return your original investment of $100,000, and you could then do whatever you wanted with your money.

Before buying bonds, there are a couple of things to consider:

1. Are you willing to bet your investment that the company you have lent your money to will not go bankrupt?

2. If you need your principal back before the end of term, are you aware that you may get back significantly less than your original investment?

Today interest rates are historically low. People are starving for more interest so they can provide their families a better quality of life. However, it is supremely important to understand there are trade-offs for higher interest rates. Generally it requires tying money up for longer periods, taking more risks, or both. When buying bonds, the interest rates offered are generally tied to the credit quality of the company and the duration of the bond. You may know nothing about bonds in general or how they work, but you can use your good old common sense to spot a good deal or a potentially bad deal.

For example, let's compare two different "fictitious" companies that want you to lend them money.

MEGA-MART is a huge, billion-dollar corporation that has been in business for fifty years and is considered to be an extremely stable company with an excellent credit rating. MEGA-MART wants to build a new store that costs a million dollars. They are willing to pay four percent interest for twenty years on any money you are willing to lend to them (bond).

Jack's Burger Shack, on the other hand, is a small, one-location hamburger restaurant that has been in business for five years. Jack's wants to expand and build two more restaurants, which will cost $1,000,000. Jack's is willing to pay four percent interest for twenty years on any money you are willing to lend to them (bond).

So here's the test: MEGA-MART and Jack's Burger Shack are paying the exact same rate of interest (four percent) for the same amount of time (twenty years). Which company would you rather lend your money to? In this case you would simply determine which of the companies has the highest probability of paying back the loan and not going bankrupt in the next twenty years. Common sense would tell you that MEGA-MART would be the safest bet.

I have people who come into my office bragging that they have a bond that is paying a very high interest rate. My initial question is, "Why is your bond paying so much higher than other bonds right now?" Generally they say they don't know why, but it's what was recommended to them. Again, generally higher interest is obtained in one of two ways:

1. More risk

2. Longer term

So let's go back at our example. Obviously, if an investor had to lend money to MEGA-MART or Jack's Burger Shack and receives the same amount of interest for the same term, Jack's Burger Shack would never have anyone lend them money. It would simply be too risky. However, what if Jack's Burger Shack changed their terms? Now instead of paying four percent for twenty years, they said they would pay ten percent for twenty years? Wow! That is one hundred fifty percent more interest than MEGA-MART for the same term.

What just happened? It is simple: with more risk comes the potential for more return. Jack's is now paying one hundred fifty percent more interest than MEGA-MART for the same term. The key to remember here is that if Jack's goes bankrupt, they could stop paying interest and you could lose all of your original investment. The question is, "Is the risk worth the potential for higher return?" That's the type of decision you, as the consumer, have to make. The only way you can make a good decision is to have the proper explanations of how bonds work and know what your risks are.

Now that we have covered some very basic concepts of how bonds work, let's talk about how bonds are purchased and sold. You may have heard about the Bond Bubble that has been in the news. The

Bond Bubble refers to what will happen to the value of existing bonds if interest rates go up.

For example, bonds are generally sold in one-thousand-dollar increments called par value. In other words, par is the standard price for one bond. So let's assume you purchase 100 bonds or lend $100,000 to MEGA-MART in exchange for four percent interest for twenty years. Soon after you purchase your bonds, interest rates start to rise again. MEGA-MART is still trying to grow, and five years later they again are trying to borrow more money from investors to build new stores.

However, this time interest rates in our economy have risen by four percent. Now MEGA-MART is paying eight percent interest for a twenty year bond instead of the four percent they paid you just five years ago. That is not great news for you. If you were still happy with the four percent interest on your bonds and MEGA-MART was still a stable company, you may be perfectly happy. However, what happens if you need the money you lent to MEGA-MART before the twenty-year term is up?

Here is where the Bond Bubble may come into play. When bond investors want the money they lent to a company back before the term is complete, the bond must be offered for sale to other bond investors based on market prices. In other words, the bonds you bought for $1,000 each (par) could be selling on the market for greater than what you paid (premium), or they could be selling for less than what you paid (discount).

Ultimately, current interest rates will determine whether or not the bonds sell at a premium or a discount? You may have heard the saying "If interest rates go up, bond values go down." Well, let me explain what that means. Remember when you lent your money to MEGA-MART (same as buying a bond from MEGA-MART) for four percent interest? Well, now you need your money back early, so you are forced to go to the bond market (through an advisor or stock broker) to sell your bond to other investors. Remember, you are receiving $4,000 per year in interest on your bond with MEGA-MART, but since *interest rates have gone up,* MEGA-MART is now paying $8,000 per year for twenty years to new investors.

So think about this: people with new money to invest are offered two bonds from MEGA-MART: one is paying eight percent and one is paying four percent, and each bond still cost $1,000 each. Which bond would you chose? Obviously you would choose the eight percent bond.

But that does not solve your problem; you still need your money back for your bond. You can't change the terms of the bond—in other words you can't change the interest rate or the term—but you can sell your bonds for less than the $1,000 each (par) you paid for them. You may be forced to sell your bonds at a *discount.*

This is where you could find yourself in trouble when interest rates rise. Here is a rule of thumb: for every one percent increase in interest rates, the value of a bond with a twenty-year maturity decreases by eight percent. So, the MEGA-MART bond you own would have decreased by thirty-two percent due to the four percent rise in interest rates. That means your $100,000 investment may only be worth $68,000.

To summarize, if interest rates go up the value of your bonds (if you have to sell them) may go down. If interest rates go down the value of your bonds (if you have to sell them) may go up in value. Obviously, due to historically low interest rates in 2012, most people think interest rates will only go up in the future. If you own long-term bonds, just be aware that rising interest rates could drastically reduce the value of your bonds if you have to sell them.

Stock Market

Historically the stock market has been a go-to place for people to invest money. Generally there are two main sources of return or interest from a stock market investment:

1. Capital appreciation

2. Dividend income

Capital Appreciation

During the '80s and '90s, the goal of most Boomers was to achieve as much capital growth or capital appreciation as possible. In general terms, *capital appreciation* is simply the value of the asset you own increasing in value. I like to use real estate to explain capital appreciation. Let's say you purchased a home in 1980 for $50,000. The $50,000 you paid for the home would be called your "cost basis," or what you have invested.

Fast-forward twenty years to 2000. You get your home appraised, and find that the market value of your home is now $200,000. The difference between what you paid ($50,000) and the current value of the property ($200,000) is your capital appreciation. In this case, your investment would have grown or appreciated by $150,000.

This same concept applies to the stock market. The idea is to buy shares of a company for as low as possible and sell those shares for as much as possible at a future date. Sounds simple, right? Well, in the '80s and '90s, it really was simple because the market was going up. However, the 2000s were not so simple because the market lost half its value two times in ten years.

Just imagine if you had recently quit your job, and the only income you had to rely on was Social Security and a stock portfolio. Things would go fine as long as the market was going up and your portfolio was appreciating, but what if the market was going down? This problem is what spurred my business, which specializes in retirement income planning, into existence. The need to generate a constant reliable income that does not rely entirely on the market appreciating in value is what many retirees today are looking for. This specific need is what separates a financial advisor who specializes in retirement income planning from your average accumulation advisor that may be more interested in working with younger families. We will talk more about that a little later, but now let's talk about the second way investors use stocks to make money and provide an income in retirement.

Dividends

Dividends are periodic interest payments that pass through to you, the investor, based on the ongoing profits that a company generates. For example, let's say you buy stock in a company that owns rental real estate (we'll call this company RRE). Obviously, the company had to pay the current market price for each property that would ultimately be rented. Each day the value of the underlying properties could fluctuate either up or down (capital appreciation or capital loss). However, the rental income from these properties generally comes in like clockwork.

The goal is to produce a reasonably predictable amount of cash flow (income) even though the value of the underlying properties may fluctuate. Therefore, an investor in this type of company would be happy with the predictable income and not as concerned with the capital appreciation. Though the income generated from dividends may be more predictable, it's important to understand that there is still risk associated with this type of investment.

I'll use RRE as an example. In 2008, when we experienced the devastation of the real-estate market in this country, many companies that owned real estate took significant capital losses. So let's say you own RRE stock that pays a six percent dividend with a stock price of $100 per share. The dividend and the stock price is based on the value of the properties owned by RRE and the amount of rental income they're bringing in.

In 2007, RRE purchased all of their rental real estate for a million dollars. If you as the investor had purchased a thousand shares of RRE for $100 per share, you would have $100,000 invested with a dividend payment of $6,000 per year plus the hope that the underlying value of the real estate would appreciate in value.

Fast-forward one year to 2008. The real-estate market has just crumbled in front of our eyes, and the value of the rental properties RRE purchased just one year earlier for a million dollars are now only worth half a million. That is a fifty percent decrease in the capital value of the investment. However, we still have the six percent ($6,000 per year) dividend that is still paying out based on the rental income. As long as the rental income keeps coming in you may feel okay. After all, as long as the income keeps coming in, there's really nothing to worry about, right?

Well, the economic impact of the 2008–2009 crash was deep and wide. Many companies started to experience problems, and many individuals started losing jobs and income. As a result, some of these companies and individuals could no longer make their rent payments or uphold their lease obligations. What if the properties owned by RRE had tenants who were affected by this economic meltdown who simply stopped paying their rent? If they stopped paying rent, RRE may not have as much profit to pass down to the investors via dividend payments. RRE may declare that they can no longer pay six percent as a dividend, and instead they can only pay four percent or potentially not pay a dividend at all.

If you relied on the income from this investment to maintain your lifestyle, you may be stuck with a stock that has dropped in value by fifty percent *and* stopped paying an income. *Now what?* What does a person do? You still need income to live. Yet if you sell now, you will lose fifty percent of your investment and still not have an income. Here is where you may have to go back to work or get a part-time job to bring in the needed income.

Obviously this would be the worst-case scenario, yet this is a very possible outcome. Without the basic understanding of how our investments work, I believe a stress-free, happy retirement is next to impossible to achieve. However, once you understand what tools you have available to provide the income you need and you understand the associated risk, you are well on your way to enjoying that stress-free, happy retirement.

Annuities

An annuity is simply an account or an agreement between you and an insurance company in which you, the investor, deposits money in exchange for an interest rate or an immediate or future income. Annuities are among the most misunderstood financial tools available. Many people are afraid of the term *annuity* because they have the belief that once you give the insurance company your money, you lose all control, and when you die, your family gets nothing. To better understand annuities and the different ways they are used, you should first understand the four basic types of annuities and how they work.

Characteristics of Annuities

- Safety of principal (except for variable annuity)
- Tax deferral
- Future guaranteed income
- Guarantees dependent on claims-paying ability of company.

1. Immediate/life (like a pension)

2. Fixed

3. Fixed indexed

4. Variable

Immediate Annuities

I like to compare an immediate annuity to a traditional pension, which we talked about earlier. Instead of the company you retired from providing you a lifetime income, you would be giving an insurance company a lump sum of saved money in exchange for a lifetime income payment. The amount of income you receive would be based on your age and how much money you give to the company.

For example, if you purchased an immediate annuity with $100,000 in your late seventies, you could get as much as $14,000 per year for the rest of your life. But if you are in your fifties or sixties, you may get only $5,000 to $6,000 per year for the rest of your life. The main advantage to an immediate annuity is the constant, reliable monthly payment you will receive regardless of what happens to interest rates or the stock market.

There are some tax advantages with immediate annuities as well. If you have money in a *taxable now* bucket that you would like to turn into an income payment, an immediate annuity could provide a guaranteed income payment that is largely *tax free*. There is something called an annuity exclusion ratio that allows for this tax advantage.

For example, a person in her seventies could take $100,000 from a taxable now account and purchase an immediate annuity. Then potentially eighty percent of the monthly income from the immediate annuity would pay out tax free.

For people looking for income for life as well as ways to reduce their tax bills, an immediate annuity may be attractive. However, there are significant disadvantages with immediate annuities: whenever you put a lump sum of money into one of these accounts, you lose control of the money. In other words, you can't ever pull that money back out. You get income for the rest of your life, but if you want your money back the next day, you can't get it.

With most immediate annuities, income stops when you die. This could be a major problem if you have a spouse who will continue to rely on the income provided by the annuity. You can set it up to pay out to a surviving spouse, but if you do not elect the joint benefit, your spouse could end up with no income and no money. I've met many couples where the husband has a pension payment that is set up to pay for only his lifetime. If something were to happen to him a year down the road, his wife would get *nothing*.

If you want a guaranteed income for the rest of your life, and you're willing to give up control of your money, an immediate annuity can be a good way to provide a constant reliable income in retirement. If you want a guaranteed income (backed by the financial stability of the issuing company) for the rest of your life but you are *not* willing to give up control of your money, there are other annuity options available for that as well. Stay tuned!

Fixed Annuities

A fixed annuity is simply an account or an agreement between you and an insurance company in which the company promises to pay a fixed rate of interest over a fixed amount of time. Though fixed annuities aren't FDIC insured, most experts agree that fixed annuities can be safe places to save money. Generally, the longer the term you're willing to park your money, the higher interest you will receive.

Fixed Indexed Annuities

A fixed indexed annuity is primarily the same as a fixed annuity in terms of safety. The main difference is in how interest is credited. In a regular fixed annuity, the term and the rate of interest are disclosed up front. In other words, you know exactly what rate of interest you will receive. But a fixed indexed annuity's interest ties the rate of interest you will receive to the performance of a stock market index like the S&P 500.

In the mid-1990s, the stock market was one of the most popular places to invest money. Investors became accustomed to making double-digit returns every year, while a simple five-year fixed annuity might have paid only 5.5 to six percent. So, to make the normal fixed annuity more attractive, insurance companies created a new way investors could have interest credited to their accounts, called a fixed indexed annuity.

Remember that both fixed and fixed indexed annuities have principal protection and are considered to be safe. The main difference is simply the way interest is credited. A fixed indexed annuity tracks a stock market index like the S&P 500 one year at a time. Over the course of that year, if the market index goes up, the owner of a fixed indexed annuity has a declared percentage of the gain credited to his or her account. However, if the market index were to crash, the owner of the fixed indexed annuity would simply make zero percent interest in that year.

Let's assume you deposit $100,000 in a fixed indexed annuity that tracks the S&P 500. The company tells you up front that if the S&P 500 increases over the next year, you will receive only fifty percent of any gains (participation rate). Most fixed indexed annuities credit interest only one time per year on what is called an anniversary date.

So let's say your account was started on January 1. Your first anniversary date would be January 1 of the following year (This is the date that you would either have interest credited to your account or not.) Let's assume that when you opened your account on January 1, the value of the S&P 500 was 1,000 points. That value would be recorded as the starting point. Now fast-forward to January 1 one year later (anniversary date) and the value of the S&P 500 on that day was 1,200 points. Again, that value would be recorded as the ending value. Over the course of the first year, the S&P 500 increased 200 points, a twenty percent increase.

However, just because the S&P 500 went up by twenty percent does not mean that your account will be credited twenty percent. Remember, the company told you up front that you would only receive fifty percent of any gains in the index in the corresponding index year. So, fifty percent of the twenty percent increase in the S&P 500 would be ten percent. That ten percent interest would then be credited to your account and would be locked in. Once you earn interest in this account, it becomes your new principal and can't be lost due to a future market decline.

We all know that the stock market doesn't always go up; sometimes it goes down. So let's use the same scenario as above with the S&P 500 value starting at 1,000 points on January 1. However, this time when we fast-forward to our anniversary date one year later the value of the S&P 500 has dropped to 800 points, a twenty percent decrease. Remember, in a fixed indexed annuity you can never lose money due to a market decline. Therefore, in any year the S&P 500 decreases in value, the worst-case scenario for the fixed indexed annuity owner would be that they earn zero percent interest for that year. If the index goes up, you participate in the gain, and if the index goes down, you do not lose your principal or any previous gains.

The concept of the fixed indexed annuity is attractive to investors who want to keep their principal and interest safe from market decreases but want potentially better growth potential than current fixed rates on CDs or regular fixed annuities.

Variable Annuities

Variable annuities invest in baskets of stocks or bonds called sub accounts. It is your responsibility as the investor to pick the sub accounts you think will perform best. Variable annuities generally have some type of guarantee associated with them, such as a death benefit or an income benefit; however, many of those benefits come with a price. Fees inside variable annuity contracts generally range between 1.5 percent to as high as four percent. Though all of the fees are required to be disclosed in the investment disclosure paperwork provided to the client before investment, it is my experience that most people simply do not take the time to read these disclosures or they are simply overwhelmed by the information. So, I believe it is very helpful to request a specific written breakdown of all fees and charges in addition to the standard disclosure paperwork you receive before investing.

Variable annuities became popular in the 1990s due to the benefits of tax deferral. During that decade, capital gains were taxed at ordinary income tax rates. So someone that was in the thirty percent tax bracket that had $20,000 in gains from an investment would have to send the IRS $6,000 in taxes at the end of the year. However, in a variable annuity, as with all annuities, those gains could be deferred until a later date. Therefore, the investors could enjoy triple tax deferral, meaning they could make interest on their principal, their interest, and the taxable part of any gains that would have been paid in a *taxable now* account.

Unlike all the other different types of annuities, with a variable annuity you assume all the investment risk. Your principal would go up or down based upon the investment options chosen. It is up to you to make good investment decisions that will make your account grow.

So it's important for you not to confuse the safety and purpose of the different types of annuities. Remember, fixed and fixed indexed annuities provide some protection from market losses, and variable annuities are subject to market losses.

Entire books are written about the different types of annuities and all of the different details of each type of annuity. There are literally thousands of different options and features with annuity contracts. There are also many misconceptions about annuities that prevent people from considering their purpose, which is ultimately to provide guaranteed income. I am going to list some of the most common myths and questions about annuities (specifically fixed and fixed indexed annuities) as well as the truth about those misconceptions to help you better sift through what I would call terrible media coverage about annuities.

Myth/Question #1:

With fixed annuities you can't get your money out for years without huge penalties.

Fact #1

First, fixed annuities are agreements or contracts. An agreement is a mutual understanding of the rules or terms between two parties. Annuities offer all types of terms for an investor to choose. Generally there is a surrender charge period, meaning if you withdraw more than a specified amount (normally ten percent of the account's value every year), you are penalized a disclosed amount. Surrender charge periods generally range from one to twenty years though some annuities may have perpetual surrender fees. Penalties for early withdrawal typically range from one percent to twenty-five percent. However, just because there is a surrender charge period does *not* mean you do not have access to money. For example, most annuities have the following allowance for accessing money without penalty:

- Ten percent of accumulated value each year with *no penalty*.

- If confined to a hospital or nursing home for a period of 90 to 180 days, one hundred percent of the account value can be withdrawn with *no penalty*.

- If you were to pass away, one hundred percent of the accumulated value would pay to your listed beneficiaries while avoiding probate.

- At the end of the surrender charge period (one to twenty years), one hundred percent of the entire account would be available penalty free at any time.

- If you had to cash out during your surrender charge period and the disclosed, agreed-upon penalty was five percent, you could simply pay the five percent penalty and any applicable taxes and access the rest of your money at any time.

I always compare the terms and penalties of annuities to a stock market investment. If you were to purchase a stock, there is no upfront agreement of the terms. There is no disclosed penalty for early withdrawals and no rules as to what happens if you get sick or pass away. You simply get whatever the market value is at the time you need your money. So, if you invested $100,000 in the stock market, and a year later you wanted to take out all of your money, what would your penalty be? The answer is you don't know because you don't know what the market is going to do. If the market is up, no problem. But what if the market is down by thirty percent? In this case you would have a $30,000 penalty if you needed your money out. In a fixed or fixed indexed annuity, at least you know the rules up front.

Myth/Question #2:

Fixed annuities charge huge fees.

Fact #2

I would be cautious of those who say fixed annuities have high fees because they are often misinformed. In fact, many fixed annuities charge no fees at all. Variable annuities are a different story. Variable annuities have many fees that can be as high as four to five percent every year. So be very careful with variable annuities in terms of fees. However, many fixed annuities generally charge no fees.

Now, let's be up front. Insurance companies, banks, or any financial institutions for that matter are not in business to lose money. They are all in business to make a profit. So, if they do not charge fees, how do they make money? If you deposit money at a bank, they may sell you a CD that pays one percent interest (by the way, you probably did not pay a fee or commission to buy the CD). Then the bank may lend your money to other home buyers or businesses for four to twelve percent. So, if the bank pays you one percent and they lend your money to another person or business for six percent it would leave the bank with five percent to pay expenses (salaries, utilities, rent, and so on) and make profits.

An insurance company invests the money you deposit with them into a hugely diversified bond portfolio that consists of hundreds, if not thousands, of high-quality bonds that may be making an average interest of four to six percent interest. If your insurance agent sells you a fixed annuity paying two percent (by the way, you did not pay an upfront fee or commission to buy the fixed annuity), and the company is making five percent, they simply pay you your two percent. Then they have to pay expenses (paying the agent) and make a profit off the remaining three percent. That's where they make their profit.

Myth/Question #3

In a fixed annuity is my money safe? How is it protected?

Fact #3

First, it is important to clarify that annuities are not FDIC insured. The guarantees provided by the insurance company are backed by their claim-paying ability. Though there is a legal reserve system in place on a state level, the health of the company is the primary concern. These are the same companies we rely on to insure our homes and our automobiles.

Insurance companies are regulated on a state level. The state regulates how insurance companies invest their money. Most fixed annuity providers invest their money primarily in investment grade bonds and US Treasury Bonds to keep the invested money as secure as possible. The insurance company is then required by law to keep a dollar in reserve for every dollar on deposit that would have to be repaid to policyholders if they wanted to retrieve their money.

That is a 1:1 ratio. So what does that mean and why is that important? Let's compare this 1:1 ratio to a bank. A bank has the right to lend money up to nine times leverage. For example, when you deposit $100,000 in a CD at a bank, the bank could use that amount as collateral to borrow up to $900,000 from the Federal Reserve. It could then essentially loan that money out for mortgages and business loans.

This is one of the reasons banks got into so much trouble back in 2008; they were overleveraged. They had more obligations than dollars to back those obligations—kind of like not being able to make the minimum payment on a credit card. If banks were not given the opportunity to leverage money in this way, we probably would never have seen a banking crisis.

Insurance companies cannot operate that way. Remember, the insurance company has to have a dollar in reserve for every dollar in deposit. Also, most insurance companies go out and insure themselves by buying insurance from reinsurers. So, if something unexpected happens, they have an additional layer of protection.

For you to lose money with an annuity, not only would the insurance company have to default, but the bonds and investments would also have to default. Then the reinsurers would have to default, and finally the legal reserve system, which is called the state guarantee fund, would have to be exhausted. Though all of these things are possible, fixed annuities offered through insurance companies are still considered to be very conservative savings accounts by most top experts.

Although I could continue listing different myths and questions about annuities, let's move on to what I call the "bells and whistles" of today's modern annuities. These "bells and whistles" are called *riders*. *Rider* is just a technical term for a benefit provided by the insurance company to the consumer that is an addition to the basic contract or agreement. There are several different riders to choose from. For example some insurance companies offer added benefits that can be purchased by paying an additional fee. Riders are used to provide specific benefits to help people solve specific problems.

For example, some companies offer what are called guaranteed income riders which are simply guarantees made by the insurance company to provide a specified amount of income for the life of the policy owner or, if married, the life of both spouses. This type of rider has become extremely popular in the last decade due to the tremendous volatility of the stock market and record-low interest rates.

Remember, company pensions are no longer available for most Americans, so the responsibility of providing retirement income falls directly on each of us. A guaranteed income rider can be used to provide a pension-like income for people who want additional income to supplement their quality of life. There are hundreds of different companies that offer guaranteed income riders, and most of the companies offer different income amounts. Most of the time there is an additional cost for these riders that generally range from zero percent to as high as two percent per year. Choosing the right rider and company for your situation is supremely important, as it could make the difference of thousands of dollars per year in additional income. So make sure you consult with an expert in income planning to find the best rider for your situation.

There are more investment tools than I can possibly list in this book, but I hope this chapter has provided a general overview of the most basic types of investments and savings plans. The world is filled with risks and problems that must be faced when it comes to money. We have to constantly combat inflation, low interest rates, the lack of company pensions, market volatility, and constantly increasing health care cost. It is my mission to help people across the country conquer their financial enemies and provide themselves a stress-free, happy retirement.

CHAPTER 6

The Stress-Free ... Happy Retirement Process

Definitions

Stress-Free: *to be without anxiety, pressure, and insecurity*

+

Happy: *feelings of enjoyment, pleasure, and satisfaction*

+

Retirement: *the phase of life when a person's income from working is replaced by income coming from other sources*

I never intended to become a financial advisor. In fact, I knew nothing about investments or money other than the fact that I had neither. I wanted to be a basketball coach like my dad. I ended up joining the Army to help pay for college and ultimately became an Army officer. When I graduated from college in December of 2001, the Army had plans to send me to Officer School in December 2002, one year later. The year between college graduation and Officer School would ultimately change the direction of my life forever.

During the year between college graduation and Officer School I decided to learn about money and investments. Little did I know that this glitch in my life would lead me to where I am today. Over the course of that year I spent hundreds of hours educating myself about investments, taxes, and insurance. I ended up passing the exams required to become licensed to offer securities and acquired multiple state insurance licenses which gave me the opportunity to assist other people in investing and protecting their money.

After graduating from Officer School I started my first job at a large brokerage company. At this point I had no "real life" experience. All of my knowledge was garnered from books. I was licensed to invest in all sorts of financial products including stocks, bonds, and mutual funds to brokerage CDs, but I knew very little about how to use these tools properly. I almost solely relied on peers and managers who had twenty-plus years of experience to show me the ropes. Most of the older guys had built their businesses on helping people grow their money. Remember, pensions were largely gone, and the individual had the responsibility to save and grow their money for the future. So growth was priority number one.

In the '80s and '90s, the market was growing, rapidly achieving double-digit returns for two decades in a row. This growth was driven largely by the 76,000,000 Baby Boomers all saving and investing for growth. Safety of principal and risk of loss were of very little concern during this time.

So, as a new investment professional, I was learning how to run an investment business designed for growth and accumulation with little concern for safety. In the early 2000s, our economy suffered some significant setbacks. We experienced the bursting of the Dot-Com bubble with technology stock imploding. On September 11, 2001, our nation was shaken by the attacks on the World Trade Center. Families who had been saving money and investing so they could someday stop working were facing the reality that their life savings had been cut in half in a very short time. Now these families were looking to their brokers to help them make good decisions about what to do during this time of volatility and transition.

Just think about this situation. Many clients had been with the same broker for years and had done very well. The market was going up; clients were making money; and brokers were making money by managing their clients' investments. However, their client bases were aging and getting closer and closer to that phase when they could no longer afford to lose what they had. They were moving from a growth and accumulation phase of their lives to a more defensive, stable phase.

However, few had the foresight to know that the market was going to experience such large losses. As a result, most brokers carried on with business as usual. They were making recommendations to not panic and simply stay on course because things would ultimately recover. Some took that advice and some did not.

Now, there I was, a new financial professional starting my business one short year after so many families had just experienced devastating losses in their portfolios. I was meeting clients every day who were trying to figure out which direction to take with their retirement dollars, and they were looking to me to give them wise counsel. Obviously I was looking for advice from experienced advisors who had been in business for many years to help confirm that the same way of investing in the past was going to continue to work in the future. After all, many of these advisors had been very successful for the past twenty years and had done very well in the '80s and '90s. I felt that I was not sophisticated enough about investments to do anything different.

So I followed the traditional way of thinking about investments by recommending stocks, bonds, and mutual funds. After meeting with hundreds of people who were getting closer and closer to retirement and continuing to invest as they had in the '80s and '90s, I started to question the wisdom in allowing my clients to be exposed to the same type of volatility that they had just experienced a year before. I felt that the investments themselves were not the problem; the investments were just tools. It was the lack of *time* that was the real problem.

As you get closer to retirement (pre-retirement), your focus must shift from growth to preservation and income. Time is simply not on your side with a volatile investment. If a significant loss occurs, it may take years to recover. My clients were looking to me for guidance and recommendations that would protect their interests and ultimately their ability to retire comfortably. I was constantly nervous knowing that my clients' fate depended on the market going up. But what was stopping the market from experiencing another 2001–2002? How was I going to protect my clients?

That's when I started aggressively researching new ideas and methods for helping my clients prepare for a stress-free, happy retirement. Over the next few years, I met with top experts in different areas of investing and honed in on what I believe are the most important aspects of preparing for retirement. My mission was to find a better way to help people entering the pre-retirement phase of their lives so they could ultimately enjoy a stress-free, happy retirement. After hundreds of hours of study and research, I established what I call the Stress-Free … Happy Retirement process.

In Chapter 1, we discussed the seven simple steps to financial freedom:

1. Educate yourself about how money works.

2. Pay yourself before you pay anyone else (except God).

3. Do *not* spend more than you make.

4. Pay off debt as fast as you can.

5. Invest the money you pay yourself so it will provide a future income and will not be lost.

6. Buy insurance to protect the things you cannot afford to lose.

7. Trust yourself to make a good decision.

I assume you have taken the time to educate yourself about different areas of investing or have hired someone to help you. I also assume that you have been diligent in paying yourself every month, avoiding debt, and living within your means. It is likely, if you have followed the seven simple steps above, you have acquired a good deal of money and may be getting closer and closer to retirement.

If you are five to ten years away from retirement, you are officially in the pre-retirement phase of life. As mentioned previously, this is the time that it is absolutely crucial to make good decisions about your money. This is the phase of life that will ultimately determine if you will be able to enjoy a stress-free, happy retirement or if you will have to continue to work.

When it comes to financial planning, there are six traditional steps associated with the planning process itself:

1. Establish financial goals. (What do you want?)

2. Gather relevant data. (Record all of your assets, debts, insurance coverage, and so on.)

3. Analyze the data. (Do basic calculations based on your goals and assumptions to determine the probability of reaching your goals.)

4. Develop a plan for achieving goals. (Do basic calculations to determine what you need to do to achieve your goals.)

5. Implement the plan. (Make a decision and follow your plan.)

6. Monitor the plan. (Financial planning is based on assumptions. You must monitor you plan to see how accurate your assumptions were. If your assumptions were not accurate, you must adjust and move on.)

This six-step financial planning process is simply a list of common-sense steps to follow while planning for the future. However, on the most basic level, most people are looking for similar things. They are looking to have security and a lifestyle that makes them happy. The six- step financial planning process is a common sense guide to retirement planning. However, we have expounded upon the six-step process and have added four distinct steps we believe are the keys to experiencing a successful retirement.

Now let's examine the four steps of the Stress-Free ... Happy Retirement philosophy.

1. Secure and maximize consistent, reliable income that will replace your current paycheck from work.

2. Do *not lose money*.

3. Buy insurance to protect you life's work.

4. Spend with confidence and trust yourself.

1. Secure and Maximize Your Sources of Guaranteed Income

This first step is probably the most important. Today the only source of reliable guaranteed retirement income for most people is Social Security. Although Social Security alone is normally not enough to provide a retirement lifestyle that is both happy and stress-free, doesn't it make sense to get the highest amount of Social Security income that you can? During your working career you paid thousands and thousands of dollars into the Social Security Trust Fund so when you become eligible, you can have a guaranteed paycheck.

I have found that most people do very little in terms of planning to get the most income they can from Social Security. They apply for Social Security when they are tired of working and want to retire. However, this could be a very costly mistake, potentially costing hundreds of thousands of dollars in lost benefits over a lifetime. It is very difficult to know the answers to common questions like these:

- When should you apply?

- Which spouse should apply first?

- Should we use the file-and-suspend method?

- What is the break-even point if we wait to file until age seventy?

- What if we die before we get our benefits?

With thousands and thousands of claiming combinations, it is next to impossible for the average American to calculate the best way to take Social Security. Though there are many free Social Security calculators out there, most of the time you get what you pay for.

So, when it comes to Social Security, it could literally pay you to get professional advice to help maximize your benefits.

After you have maximized your Social Security benefits, you will need to determine if the Social Security amount alone is enough to provide a stress-free, happy-retirement lifestyle. If the answer to that question is, "No." that simply means you need more guaranteed income. So where do you go to get more guaranteed income? This is where your savings will come into play. The money that you have saved over the years in your 401k or IRA or savings account will need to be invested to provide a level of income that would allow you to live the stress-free, happy retirement you desire.

In the previous chapter, we talked about the four basic types of investments or savings accounts that people can use to help provide the lifestyle they want. However, I am a strong believer in using an annuity account to provide a guaranteed reliable source of income for retirement.

For example, if a seventy-year-old male wants to purchase a private pension that provides $1,000 per month in income for the rest of his life, it would cost him approximately $200,000. So let's assume that this individual has a $500,000 portfolio. He could simply carve out $200,000 to provide the guaranteed income he desires that would pay out to him no matter what happened to the stock market or interest rates.

He would then be left with $300,000 to invest in dividend-paying stocks, bonds, real estate, or whatever other investment he chooses. The key here is as long as this individual invests a portion of his money to provide a level of income that will provide the stress-free, happy retirement he wants, it really does not matter what happens to the rest of the portfolio.

Just imagine the power you have to control the level of guaranteed retirement income you receive, no matter what happens in the economy. My happiest clients are not the ones with the most money; they are the ones with the most amount of guaranteed income. They spend money freely without the worry of running out of money. They know that every month they can expect a deposit in their bank account or a check in the mail. The best part of my job is when a client takes a big, deep breath and says, "I am so glad we don't have to worry about spending money anymore."

2. Do *Not* Lose Money

This step is simple. Let's face it; *stress-free* and *happy* are not terms that come to mind when you lose money. It may have taken a lifetime to save that money, and didn't you save it so you would get to use it and enjoy it later? If you feel like you have to invest in risky investments to maintain your retirement lifestyle, the bottom line is you probably were not ready to retire in the first place.

I have seen people's lives completely unravel because they chose to invest money they were relying on to provide retirement income in volatile investments. Life is great as long as the market is going up, but when the season changes and the portfolio starts losing value, it can snowball into a major problem. In the last decade, ten years of gains have been completely wiped out in as little as ten months. It simply makes good business sense not to lose money that has taken a lifetime to accumulate.

3. Buy Insurance to Protect Your Life's Work

There are all kinds of different types of protection you could buy to safeguard various areas of your life.

- Life insurance

- Car Insurance

- Health insurance

- Homeowner's insurance

- Home security systems

- Long-term care insurance

- Smoke detectors

- Disability insurance

- Storm cellars

- And others

The whole purpose of insurance is to protect the things we don't want to use our own money to replace. Though we may have to pay a monthly or annual insurance premium for protection, the peace of mind and comfort that monthly premium provides can be wonderful. I told you the story of my recent house fire and the feeling of peace I had knowing I had insurance to protect my home. I think of insurance as armor against financial ruin.

One of the things my clients comment to me about most is the fact that when they had nothing, they did not need insurance to protect anything. Now that they have saved and accumulated assets, they must buy insurance or a suit of armor to protect what they have accumulated. This seems cruel, but this is just how the game is played. It seems that people who do not really need much insurance are either the super wealthy or the poor. The super wealthy have enough money to pay to replace most of their assets, and the poor simply have nothing to protect. It is the average person with assets between $100,000 and $2,000,000 who needs insurance protection the most.

I have found that the people who have bought insurance protection to cover the areas that could cause them financial ruin are the most stress-free, happy clients I have. Everyone else is simply gambling. They are betting their life's work that something catastrophic will not happen to them. Funny, I *never* thought *my* house would catch on fire, but it did. I am glad I had insurance.

Spend Money with Confidence and Trust Yourself

Some people keep themselves up at night worrying due to a lack of financial education and planning. However, with knowledge comes power. Once you have educated yourself about how money works, you have sought out professional advice when needed, and you have developed a plan for success, it is time to stop worrying. Now you have provided yourself with the power to spend money with confidence and to be happy. Life is so uncertain; we never know what day on Earth will be our last. So take advantage of the time you have and have fun. I met an older couple a few years ago who really changed the way I look at money and retirement. They had both been previously married for over thirty years before losing their spouses. They said that the one thing they regretted most was not taking the time to enjoy life with their previous spouses while they still had them.

When this couple met and decided to get married, they made a pact that they would do things differently this time. First, they decided to invest their money to generate guaranteed income that would be paid to them for the rest of both of their lives. Second, they decided to invest their money so they would not lose it. They both agreed that they had reached a point in their lives where the return *of* their money was more important than the return *on* their money. And finally they bought insurance to protect their life's savings from nursing homes and market losses. Now, they do not worry about low interest rates, or the ups and downs of the stock market, or constantly worrying if they are going to run out of money. Now they spend their time planning vacations and having fun. They are living stress-free, happy lives.

I encourage you to continually seek out knowledge and prepare yourself for your life's financial game. I believe that if you follow the simple principles in this book and you follow the four simple steps of the Stress-Free … Happy Retirement process, you will find great financial success.

I have intentionally not talked about specific strategies and investment details in this book, as everyone's situation is unique. The strategies and specific investments I pick for the families I represent are tailored to their specific goals and comfort levels.

My hope is that this book has provided some simple yet powerful concepts that you can use to make better financial decisions in the future. Obviously, concepts and ideas are worthless without action. So, I challenge you to take action so you too can enjoy a more stress free, happy retirement.

QUESTIONS TO HELP UNDERSTAND HOW TO MAKE YOUR FINANCIAL LIFE MORE STRESS FREE AND HAPPY

Values:

a. *What do you need your money to do for you to make you happy for the rest of your life?*

_____

_____

_____

_____

_____

b. *How important is it to have a financial road map that will steer you throughout your life so you can make good financial decisions?*

_____

_____

_____

_____

Do you currently have this roadmap?

_____

_____

c. *How important is it to you to prevent your investments from suffering significant losses?*

_____

_____

Does your current investment portfolio reflect your feelings toward losses?

_____

_____

d. *How important is it to receive a consistent, reliable monthly income from your investments that you can spend and enjoy for the rest of your lives without the fear of running out of money?*

_____

_____

Do you currently have a plan to provide this type of income?

_____

e. How important is it that your kids and grandkids are left with an inheritance that minimizes taxes and avoids probate costs?

_____

_____

Do you currently have a plan to accomplish this?

_____

_____

f. Are there any other financial areas that you would like to improve?

_____

_____

_____

_____

_____

_____

Business Relationship:

g. Are you a Master Investor, Worker, or Protector?

_____

_____

_____

h. *If you consider working with a financial advisor, what would you want them to do to help make your financial life better?*

_____

_____

_____

_____

i. *If you were meeting with your advisor three years from today, what would you have had to accomplish during that time for you to be happy?*

_____

_____

_____

_____

j. *If you work with a financial advisor, in what ways and how often would you like them to keep you informed about your progress?*

_____

_____

_____

_____

NOTES

www.ingramcontent.com/pod-product-compliance
Lightning Source LLC
Chambersburg PA
CBHW022101170526
45157CB00004B/1430